The salvaged mainmast of the battleship *Maine* stands as a memorial to the dead at Arlington National Cemetery, Virginia.

Twisted wreckage of the *Maine* in Havana Harbor, February 15, 1898

Cornerstones of Freedom

The Story of DISCARD

THE SINKING OF THE BATTLESHIP MAINE

By Zachary Kent

CHILDRENS PRESS®

CHICAGO

The *Maine* explodes in a fiery blast.

Library of Congress Cataloging-in-Publication Data

Kent, Zachary.
     The story of the sinking of the battleship Maine / by Zachary Kent.
        p.   cm. — (Cornerstones of freedom)
     Summary: Discusses the mysterious sinking of the battleship
Maine and the subsequent involvement of the United States in the
Spanish-American War.
     ISBN 0-516-04736-1
     1.   *Maine* (Battleship) — Juvenile literature.   2.   United States-
-Politics and government — War of 1898 — Juvenile literature.
3.   United States — History — War of 1898 — Causes — Juvenile literature.
[1.   *Maine* (Battleship)   2.   United States — History — War of 1898.]
I.   Title.   II.   Series.   87-35465
E721.6.K46   1988   CIP
973.8'9 — dc19   AC

Childrens Press®, Chicago
Copyright ©1988 by Regensteiner Publishing Enterprises, Inc.
All rights reserved. Published simultaneously in Canada.
Printed in the United States of America.
1 2 3 4 5 6 7 8 9 10 R 97 96 95 94 93 92 91 90 89 88

The United States battleship *Maine* rocked gently at her mooring place in the harbor of Havana, Cuba on February 15, 1898. On deck the night lookouts quietly patroled, while down below sleepy crew-members climbed into their hammocks. Seated at his cabin desk, Captain Charles Sigsbee calmly wrote a letter to his wife. He paused and listened as a bugler blew the notes of taps.

Minutes later the dreaminess of the hot, tropical night turned into a nightmare. At 9:40 P.M. a sudden, roaring explosion jolted the *Maine* half out of the water. The fiery blast hurled metal fragments of the ship high into the air. Burned and bloodied sailors screamed in agony as water rushed through the ruined hull. Staggering down a smoke-filled corridor Captain Sigsbee hurried onto deck.

"What is it?" he yelled to the first man he saw.

"I think the ship has blown up, sir," answered a dazed marine.

Officers and enlisted men battled half a dozen fires as ammunition below deck continued to burst and crackle. Staring past the flames Captain Sigsbee discovered the forward half of the *Maine* already had disappeared under the water.

"Abandon ship!" he ordered.

Survivors clambered into lifeboats. In another five minutes the *Maine* sank down into the harbor mud. Only smokestacks, masts, and wreckage

$50,000 REWARD.—WHO DESTROYED THE MAINE?—$50,000 REWARD.

EDITION FOR GREATER NEW YORK.

NEW YORK JOURNAL
AND ADVERTISER.

The Journal will give $50,000 for information, furnished to it exclusively, that will convict the person or persons who sank the Maine.

The Journal will give $50,000 for information, furnished to it exclusively, that will convict the person or persons who sank the Maine.

NO. 3,572.   Copyright, 1898, by W. R. Hearst.—NEW YORK, THURSDAY, FEBRUARY 17, 1898.—16 PAGES.   PRICE ONE CENT In Greater New York and Jersey City; Elsewhere, TWO CENTS.

DESTRUCTION OF THE WAR SHIP MAINE WAS THE WORK OF AN ENEMY.

$50,000!

$50,000 REWARD!
For the Detection of the Perpetrator of the Maine Outrage!

The New York Journal hereby offers a reward of $50,000 CASH for information, FURNISHED TO IT EXCLUSIVELY, which shall lead to the detection and conviction of the person, persons or government criminally responsible for the explosion which resulted in the destruction, at Havana, of the United States war ship Maine and the loss of 258 lives of American sailors.

The $50,000 CASH offered for the above information is on deposit with Wells, Fargo & Co.

No one is barred, be he the humble but misguided seaman eking out a few miserable dollars by acting as a spy, or the attache of a government secret service, plotting, by any devilish means, to revenge fancied insults or cripple menacing countries.

This offer has been cabled to Europe and will be made public in every capital of the Continent and in London this morning.

The Journal believes that any man who can be bought to commit murder can also be bought to betray his comrades. FOR THE PERPETRATOR OF THIS OUTRAGE HAD ACCOMPLICES.

W. R. HEARST.

Assistant Secretary Roosevelt Convinced the Explosion of the War Ship Was Not an Accident.

The Journal Offers $50,000 Reward for the Conviction of the Criminals Who Sent 258 American Sailors to Their Death. Naval Officers Unanimous That the Ship Was Destroyed on Purpose.

$50,000!

$50,000 REWARD!
For the Detection of the Perpetrator of the Maine Outrage!

The New York Journal hereby offers a reward of $50,000 CASH for information, FURNISHED TO IT EXCLUSIVELY, which shall lead to the detection and conviction of the person, persons or government criminally responsible for the explosion which resulted in the destruction, at Havana, of the United States war ship Maine and the loss of 258 lives of American sailors.

The $50,000 CASH offered for the above information is on deposit with Wells, Fargo & Co.

No one is barred, be he the humble but misguided, woman, eking out a few miserable dollars by acting as a spy, or the attache of a government secret service, plotting, by any devilish means, to revenge fancied insults or cripple menacing countries.

This offer has been cabled to Europe and will be made public in every capital of the Continent and in London this morning.

The Journal believes that any man who can be bought to commit murder can also be bought to betray his comrades. FOR THE PERPETRATOR OF THIS OUTRAGE HAD ACCOMPLICES.

W. R. HEARST.

POWDER MAGAZINE

NAVAL OFFICERS THINK THE MAINE WAS DESTROYED BY A SPANISH MINE.

George Eugene Bryson, the Journal's special correspondent at Havana, cables that it is the secret opinion of many Spaniards in the Cuban capital that the Maine was destroyed and 258 of her men killed by means of a submarine mine, or fixed torpedo. This is the opinion of several American naval authorities. The Spaniards, it is believed, arranged to have the Maine anchored over one of the harbor mines. Wires connected the mine with a powder magazine, and it is thought the explosion was caused by sending an electric current through the wire. If this can be proven, the brutal nature of the Spaniards will be shown by the fact that they waited to spring the mine until after all the men had retired for the night. The Maltese cross in the picture shows where the mine may have been fired.

Hidden Mine or a Sunken Torpedo Believed to Have Been the Weapon Used Against the American Man-of-War---Officers and Men Tell Thrilling Stories of Being Blown Into the Air Amid a Mass of Shattered Steel and Exploding Shells---Survivors Brought to Key West Scout the Idea of Accident---Spanish Officials Protest Too Much---Our Cabinet Orders a Searching Inquiry---Journal Sends Divers to Havana to Report Upon the Condition of the Wreck. Was the Vessel Anchored Over a Mine?

BY CAPTAIN E. L. ZALINSKI, U. S. A.

(Captain Zalinski is the inventor of the famous dynamite gun, which would be the principal factor in our coast defence in case of war.)

Assistant Secretary of the Navy Theodore Roosevelt says he is convinced that the destruction of the Maine in Havana Harbor was not an accident. The Journal offers a reward of $50,000 for exclusive evidence that will convict the person, persons or Government criminally responsible for the destruction of the American battle ship and the death of 258 of its crew.

The suspicion that the Maine was deliberately blown up grows stronger every hour. Not a single fact to the contrary has been produced.

Captain Sigsbee, of the Maine, and Consul-General Lee both urge that public opinion be suspended until they have completed their investigation. They are taking the course of tactful men who are convinced that there has been treachery.

Washington reports very late that Captain Sigsbee had feared some such event as a hidden mine. The English cipher code was used all day yesterday by the naval officers in cabling instead of the usual American code.

remained above the water's surface. Of the crew of 354 men, a shocking 266 had been killed or drowned.

For three years Cuban freedom fighters had been in revolt against their Spanish rulers. The *Maine* had sailed to Havana to protect American citizens living there. Now the disastrous sinking of the battleship thrust the United States into the Cuban conflict. "DESTRUCTION OF THE WARSHIP *MAINE* WAS THE WORK OF AN ENEMY," blared one New York newspaper headline. Many Americans blamed Spain for the mysterious explosion. In cities and towns across the nation people loudly chanted the slogan: "Remember the *Maine*! To hell with Spain!" This fierce call for quick revenge hurtled the United States headlong into the Spanish-American War.

The end of the 1890s marked the close of an era in United States history. For over a century hardy, restless American settlers had pushed across the continent taming the wilderness. By 1890 the sound of the ax filled the nation's forests and farmers tilled the plains where herds of bison once roamed. In growing towns and cities the machinery of factories thumped and whined, and every day new immigrants crowded the streets eager to find work. From the Atlantic to the Pacific, America was booming, and having filled its natural boundaries it searched for new frontiers.

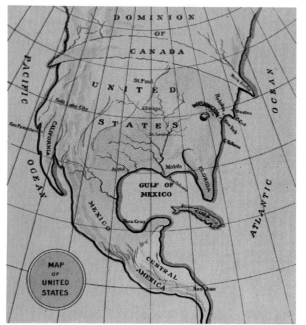

The 1898 cartoon (left) shows the United States about to swallow Cuba. The cartoon (right) depicts President McKinley bullying King Alfonso XIII of Spain.

Senator Albert J. Beveridge of Indiana voiced the feelings of most Americans: "... we are a conquering race ... we must obey our blood and occupy new markets, and if necessary new lands." England, France, Germany, and Spain possessed territory in every corner of the world. With patriotic fervor the United States wished to join these great European nations as a world power. The Washington *Post* reported, "The taste of Empire is in the mouth of the people."

In 1893 the United States encouraged the overthrow of the queen of Hawaii. Five years later the government formally claimed those distant Pacific islands as U.S. territory. Much closer to home Americans keenly followed activities in Cuba. Since the days of Christopher Columbus, Spain had governed Cuba located just ninety miles south of Florida. Tired of harsh Spanish rule, however, in 1895 the Cuban people rose up in open revolt.

With guns and sharp machetes Cuban rebels called *insurrectos* attacked Spanish army outposts. Charging out of the jungles, Cuban raiders burned villages, destroyed sugar plantations, and wrecked railroad depots. In response Spanish soldiers built blockhouses, dug trenches, and strung barbed wire across the Cuban countryside. In its brutal effort to conquer the *insurrectos* the Spanish made arrests, tortured citizens, and executed suspected rebels. Yelling *Cuba Libre!* (Free Cuba!) many Americans showed which side they favored in this struggle.

Two rival New York City newspapers took quick advantage of American interest in the Cuban war. The New York *Journal* owned by William Randolph Hearst and the New York *World* owned by Joseph Pulitzer were in stiff competition for readers. To attract attention, both papers used giant headlines, placed eye-catching illustrations on their front pages, and printed sensational news stories. Both papers published a popular cartoon called "The Yellow Kid" and soon their gaudy style of reporting became known as "yellow journalism."

Crowds at Newspaper Row in New York City await current news
of the Spanish-American War.

As Americans clamored for news, the newspapers
hurried reporters to Havana. Early in 1896 these
newsmen learned of Spanish general Valeriano
Weyler's ruthless new *reconcentrado* policy. To cut
off the rebels from food and supplies, Spanish
soldiers herded thousands of Cuban peasants into
concentration camps. In these prisons starvation and
disease killed many men, women, and children.

United States newspapers labeled General Weyler "the Butcher." To fuel excitement among Americans the yellow press printed wilder stories every day. "FEEDING PRISONERS TO SHARKS," screamed one *Journal* headline condemning savage Spanish troops. The *World* soon printed a story that described Cuba as a place with "blood on the roadsides, blood in the fields, blood on the doorsteps, blood, blood, blood!" Whether true or false, across the United States people snapped up newspapers to read spectacular stories of gallant *insurrectos*, cruel Spaniards, and bloody violence.

Maps showing the location of points being held by Spanish forces appeared in most newspapers of the day.

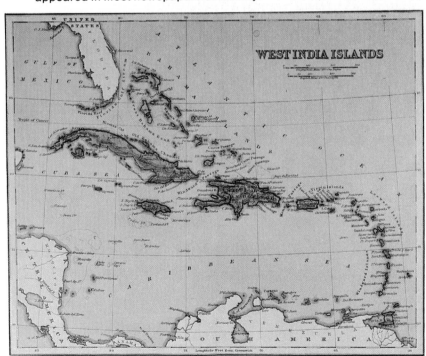

In January 1897 the *Journal* sent Frederic Remington to Cuba to draw pictures of the action. Remington discovered that there was a lull in the fighting. He telegraphed Hearst, "Everything is quiet. There is no trouble. There will be no war. I wish to return." Peace in Cuba would not sell newspapers, so Hearst promptly wired back, ". . . You furnish the pictures and I'll furnish the war."

In time relations between the United States and Spain grew more strained. On January 12, 1898 Spanish soldiers rioted in Havana. They charged through the streets smashing windows, looting stores, and setting fires. The United States consul to Havana, Fitzhugh Lee, worried about the safety of American citizens living in Cuba. "Americans and their interests are in danger. . . . Ships must be sent . . ." he hurriedly telegraphed the U.S. State Department. In an effort to ease tensions, President William McKinley ordered the battleship *Maine* to Havana to make a "good will" visit.

On the morning of January 25, 1898 the *Maine* steamed into Havana Harbor. The hull of the great 6,682-ton warship was painted white. Along her 319-foot deck two tall masts and two smoke funnels thrust up into the sky. Sailors dressed in white stood beside four powerful ten-inch guns and six six-inch guns. Greatly impressed, throngs of people crowded

the Havana waterfront and watched the *Maine* drop anchor at her assigned mooring place.

"OUR FLAG IN HAVANA AT LAST!" joyfully exclaimed the New York *Journal* soon afterward. Some Americans worried that the warship's presence in Havana might cause trouble. Senator Mark Hanna of Ohio believed it was like "waving a match in an oil well." For three weeks, though, Havana remained calm and the *Maine* rested peacefully in the harbor.

On the evening of February 15, 1898 several American newspaper reporters sat relaxing at a

Havana café. Across the darkened harbor they recognized the dim outline of the *Maine* and heard the sleepy bugle notes of taps. Thirty minutes later a terrific explosion rocked them in their seats. Rushing to the waterfront they discovered the *Maine* engulfed in flames and sinking. Bursting ammunition lit the sky with stunning fireworks.

Newsman George Rea declared, "The scene ...was terrible.... Great masses of twisted and bent iron plates and beams were thrown up in confusion amidships; the bow had disappeared; the foremast and smoke stacks had fallen ..." Only pieces of jagged metal poked above the water. The main

The remains of the sunken *Maine*

explosion had occurred at the forward part of the ship. Sadly that was where most of the enlisted sailors slept. Through the night rescue boats frantically searched the harbor for survivors. Clara Barton, president of the American Red Cross, was already in Havana to distribute food to starving Cubans. She rushed to the city's hospitals to help the injured sailors in any way she could.

Within a few hours Captain Sigsbee wired Washington: "*Maine* blown up in Havana harbor at nine-forty to-night and destroyed. Many wounded and doubtless more killed or drowned. . . . Public opinion should be suspended until further report." The cause of the disaster was still unknown. Shocked Americans, however, aroused by lurid newspaper reports, quickly blamed the Spanish.

"THE WARSHIP MAINE WAS SPLIT IN TWO BY AN ENEMY'S SECRET INFERNAL MACHINE," shrieked the New York *Journal*. That newspaper claimed Spanish spies had planted a bomb in the *Maine's* boiler room. The New York *World* insisted the Spanish had placed an exploding mine in the water under the *Maine's* bow.

"THE WHOLE COUNTRY THRILLS WITH THE WAR FEVER," blared the *Journal*. "REMEMBER THE MAINE! WAR NOW!" raged the *World*. Newspaper sales skyrocketed as Americans whipped themselves into a fury.

Theodore Roosevelt

President William McKinley

President McKinley hoped to find a peaceful solution to the Cuba crisis. A veteran of the American Civil War, McKinley already had seen enough bloodshed in his lifetime. "I detest war," he proclaimed. "There never has been a good war or a bad peace." In his 1895 inaugural address he had stated, "We want no wars of conquest; we must avoid the temptation of territorial aggression."

Most Americans, though, were itching for a fight. Theodore Roosevelt, the brash thirty-nine-year-old assistant secretary of the Navy complained that McKinley had "no more backbone than a chocolate eclair." "We will have this war for the freedom of Cuba," he insisted, "in spite of . . . timidity." Other war hawks echoed Roosevelt's opinions.

President McKinley ordered a U.S. Navy commission to investigate the *Maine* sinking. In Havana Harbor navy divers examined the twisted wreckage. Navy engineers scribbled opinions and a court of inquiry interviewed survivors and sifted through the evidence. On March 25 the court submitted its report. It declared that "the *Maine* was destroyed by the explosion of two or more of the forward magazines. . . . The court has been unable to obtain evidence fixing the responsibility for the destruction of the *Maine* upon any person or persons."

Angry Americans formed their own opinions. "DESTRUCTION OF THE MAINE BY FOUL PLAY," trumpeted the New York *World*, adding: ". . . we must punish Spain." "I have no more doubt than I am now standing in the Senate of the United States," declared Massachusetts Senator Henry Cabot Lodge, "that that ship was blown up by a government mine, fired by, or with the connivance of, Spanish officials." Caving in at last to public pressure, on April 11 President McKinley asked Congress to grant him war powers. Amid patriotic songs and cheering on April 25, 1898 Congress declared war against Spain.

President McKinley called for 125,000 army volunteers, and thrilled Americans prepared themselves for war. Kansas newspaper editor William Allen White exclaimed, "In April, everywhere over this good, fair land, flags were flying. Trains carry-

Woman recruiting officer

ing soldiers were hurrying . . . and as they sped over the green prairies and the brown mountains, little children on fences greeted soldiers with flapping scarfs and handkerchiefs and flags; at the stations, crowds gathered to hurrah for the soldiers, and to throw hats into the air, and to unfurl flags. Everywhere it was flags: tattered smoke-grimed flags in engine cabs; flags in buttonholes; flags on proud poles; flags fluttering everywhere."

Teddy Roosevelt and his "Rough Riders"

Theodore Roosevelt resigned his government position and eagerly accepted an army commission as a lieutenant colonel. In San Antonio, Texas he whipped together an unusual cavalry regiment made up of lean cowboys, sharpshooting Indians, and Ivy League college athletes. Newspapermen called this hardy unit of volunteers names like "Teddy's Terrors" and "Teddy's Riotous Rounders," until the colorful name "Roosevelt's Rough Riders" stuck.

Admiral George Dewey at Manila Bay, from a painting by R. F. Zogbaum

While the War Department scrambled to collect guns, ammunition, food, and uniforms for its inexperienced army, a U.S. naval squadron under Commodore George Dewey steamed into immediate action. The Philippine Islands in the Pacific belonged to Spain. Commodore Dewey intended to attack the Spanish fleet anchored in Manila Bay. In the morning blackness of May 1, 1898 the American cruisers arrived at the fortified entrance to the bay.

"We're sticking our necks in a noose," one officer warned Dewey. He described the dangers of explosive mines, land-based cannon, and the waiting Spanish fleet, adding, "I fear the outcome of this mission . . ."

"As do I," replied the crusty, sixty-year-old naval commander. "But I have my orders and shall carry them out at any cost."

From mountain forts Spanish cannon roared as the U.S. ships sped into the bay. The guns of the Spanish fleet boomed and belched flame as the enemy steamed close. At 5:45 A.M. Commodore Dewey turned to the captain of his flagship *Olympia* and calmly ordered: "You may fire when ready, Gridley."

The great guns of Dewey's squadron hammered away. Firing through the clouds of smoke, the American gunners proved most effective. By noon all of the Spanish ships were destroyed, driven aground, burning, or sinking. The Spaniards lost 381 men killed or injured. Only eight U.S. sailors needed bandaging for slight wounds.

When news of this incredible victory reached the United States, Americans cheered and danced in the streets. Dewey was quickly promoted to admiral and the public made him the hero of the day. Dewey dolls, Dewey toys, Dewey hats, and Dewey buttons instantly appeared for sale. A candy company invented a gum called Dewey's Chewies, and one poet proudly wrote:

"Oh, dewy was the morning,

Upon the first of May.

And Dewey was the admiral

Down in Manila Bay.

And dewy were the Spaniards' eyes,

Them orbs of black and blue.

And dew we feel discouraged?

I dew not think we dew!"

The ships of Spain's remaining fleet sailed at top speed across the Atlantic in an effort to protect Cuba. The *Brooklyn*, *Texas*, *Iowa*, and other American warships of Commodore Winfield Scott Schley's Atlantic squadron discovered the Spanish fleet at Santiago, Cuba. Immediately the U.S. ships formed a blockade and trapped the Spanish ships inside the harbor. For added security, 650 U.S.

Battle scene at Guantanamo Bay

marines soon landed at nearby Guantanamo Bay and captured that fine natural port. New York *World* reporter Stephen Crane, already famous for his Civil War novel, *The Red Badge of Courage*, followed the marines ashore and remembered "the hot hiss of the bullets trying to cut my hair."

At Tampa, Florida the U.S. Fifth Army hurriedly gathered. Many soldiers worried the war would be over before they got a chance to fight. With great confusion soldiers loaded supplies and piled onto cramped transport ships. The enlisted men of the Rough Rider cavalry regiment were forced to leave their horses behind. Finally on June 8 the convoy of 17,000 men commanded by General William Shafter steamed ahead toward Cuba.

For two weeks the troops suffered aboard the sweltering ships. At last the army reached the village of Daiquiri, eighteen miles from Santiago on the southern coast of Cuba. Two days later on June 24 the Rough Riders and two other cavalry regiments tramped inland on the jungle road to Santiago. At a ridge called Las Guasimas the Spanish lay waiting in trenches and behind trees. Suddenly the zip of Mauser bullets tore into the American columns. Cavalry general Joseph Wheeler was a veteran of the Confederate army during the American Civil War. As he rallied his soldiers around him, the excited old rebel got confused. "Come on, boys," he yelled. "We've got the damn Yankees on the run!" Although several troopers died and many more were wounded in this skirmish, the Americans charged the enemy and forced them to retreat.

In the following days the army pushed ahead to the outskirts of Santiago. Blocking the way to the north stood the fortified village of El Caney. To the west rose the San Juan Heights defended by barbed wire, trenches, and blockhouses. On the morning of July 1, 1898 General Shafter ordered attacks on El Caney and the San Juan Heights. The battle began with the fight for El Caney. Sweating in their heavy blue flannel shirts and khaki trousers the U.S. soldiers struggled to capture the village. Cannon

roared and rapid-fire Gatling guns spit bullets.
Finally the Twenty-fifth Infantry, a regiment of
black soldiers, bravely charged into the village
streets. When the smoke cleared the American flag
waved above El Caney.

At the foot of the San Juan Heights (which
included San Juan Hill to the left and Kettle Hill to
the right), many soldiers fainted from the heat while
awaiting final orders. Heavy riflefire and cannonfire
cut into their ranks and men dropped screaming
with pain. At last orders arrived to move forward.
Galloping along the battleline Colonel Roosevelt
shouted to his Rough Riders, "Follow me!" Joined
by eager black troops of the Ninth and Tenth Regiments, as well as others, Roosevelt boldly led the
charge up Kettle Hill.

Roosevelt leading the charge near San Juan Hill, from a lithograph by W. G. Read

The men surged forward, shouting and firing as they ran. "I waved my hat," Roosevelt later exclaimed, "and we went up the hill in a rush." Having a horse enabled Roosevelt to advance well ahead of his foot soldiers. Newspaperman Richard Harding Davis declared, "Roosevelt mounted high on horseback, and charging the rifle pits at a gallop and quite alone, made you feel that you would like to cheer." As the wave of soldiers swarmed close, frightened Spaniards threw down their guns and ran. Before the day was through, American troops had conquered the San Juan Heights. From this position the soldiers gazed at the rooftops of Santiago in the distance.

News of Roosevelt's valiant charge electrified the United States. The event made him even more famous than Admiral Dewey and guaranteed his political career. In another two years Americans elected the heroic Rough Rider vice president. After a crazed assassin shot President McKinley in 1901, Roosevelt became president of the United States. But he never forgot his ride up Kettle Hill which he called "the great day of my life."

Nearly surrounded now, Admiral Pascual Cervera desperately tried to save his Spanish fleet. On the morning of July 3, 1898 Cervera's four Spanish cruisers and two torpedo boats steamed out of Santiago Harbor. Aboard the *Brooklyn* Commodore Schley quickly raised signal flags: "Clear all ships for action. Engage the enemy." The giant guns of the U.S. battleships sent shells shrieking through the sky. The Spanish ships sailed on, hoping to break through the blockade, but the Americans pounded blazing broadside after broadside into their hulls. Within four hours the naval battle of Santiago ended. The Spanish fleet was totally destroyed, its battered ships sunken, beached, or burning. Spanish losses numbered 474 sailors killed or injured while only one American seaman died.

Admiral Winfield S. Schley

U. S. navy blockading Havana Harbor

"A glorious victory has been achieved," exclaimed Commodore Schley. "This is a great day for our country." In the United States, people greeted word of this latest success with screeching train whistles, clanging church bells, and banging gun salutes.

The loss of these last Spanish ships spelled the doom of Santiago and all of Cuba. Soon Spanish officers negotiated the surrender of their army. On the San Juan Heights newsman John Fox, Jr. reported, ". . . the word went around that the Spaniard had come down from his high horse. He would stack his arms, march out, evacuate the province, surrender all the troops in it—some twenty thousand. . . . The sunny air straight-away was rent with cheers. The sickest man in one regiment sprang from his blanket and led all his comrades . . . in the hallelujahs."

On August 12, 1898 fresh orders arrived from Washington: "Suspend all hostilities." The United States and Spain had declared an armistice. After only 110 days of fighting the war was over. Across the United States Americans wildly celebrated. Fifteen hundred soldiers had been killed or wounded in Cuba. Hundreds more had fallen victim to tropical diseases such as malaria and yellow fever. Still, Americans gloried in their swift and total victory.

"It's been a splendid little war," declared American diplomat John Hay, "begun with the highest motives, carried on with magnificent intelligence and spirit, favored by that fortune which loves the brave." A few people argued that it was a totally needless war, provoked by the yellow press, and won by luck. As a result of the conflict, however, the United States obtained new territories. The island of Puerto Rico in the Caribbean and the island of Guam in the Pacific became American possessions and remain so today. The important Philippine

This cartoon, which ran in the Philadelphia *Press*, shows the extent of U.S. expansion in 1898.

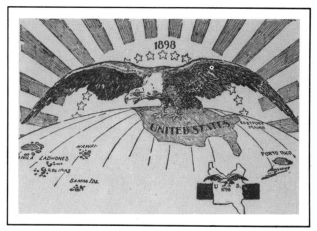

Islands also became U.S. territory (until granted independence in 1946).

Though no one could have guessed it, the sinking of the battleship *Maine* had marked a turning point in United States history. As a result of the Spanish-American War, America proudly became a world power.

In 1911 U.S. army engineers raised the wreck of the *Maine* from the mud to study it more carefully. The cause of the fateful explosion still could not be determined. New theories, though, strongly suggest that natural gases in the ship's coal bunker had ignited by accident. This explosion, in turn, blew up adjacent ammunition magazines. It is possible the Spanish were completely blameless for the fateful disaster.

The navy towed the wreck from Havana Harbor and re-sank it with solemn honors at sea. Seventy bodies recovered from the wreck were buried at Arlington National Cemetery. Today as a lasting memorial to the battleship, its salvaged mainmast stands at Arlington. At the U.S. Naval Academy at Annapolis, Maryland, its foremast still stands tall. Today naval cadets stride across campus to study the events that led America to her present greatness. Stopping to gaze at the symbolic foremast, they cannot fail to "Remember the *Maine.*"

The foremast of the battleship *Maine* at the Naval Academy
in Annapolis, Maryland

1897 lithograph of the U.S. Battleship *Maine*

About the Author

    Zachary Kent grew up in Little Falls, New Jersey, and received an English degree from St. Lawrence University. Following college he worked at a New York City literary agency for two years and then launched his writing career. To support himself while writing, he has worked as a taxi driver, a shipping clerk, and a house painter. Mr. Kent has had a lifelong interest in American history. Studying the U.S. presidents was his childhood hobby. His collection of presidential items includes books, pictures, and games, as well as several autographed letters.